W9-BYM-431

Volcano!

PIONEER EDITION

By Beth Geiger

CONTENTS

Volcanoes are some of the hottest places on Earth. They are also some of the coolest.

Volcano!

Kilauea, Hawaii

G. BRAD LEWIS. GETTY IMAGES.

By Beth Geiger

Joanne Green walks by a glowing river. This river has no water. It is made of hot rock.

Green has to be careful. The rock is blazing hot. One wrong step could melt her boots. Or worse!

Green is used to these dangers. They are part of her job. She is a scientist who studies volcanoes.

Volcanoes on Earth

Green was studying Kilauea. It is a volcano in Hawaii. Green studies other volcanoes too. Earth has thousands of volcanoes.

What exactly is a volcano? It is an opening, or vent, in Earth. Hot rock, called **magma,** rises through the vent. Soon it reaches Earth's surface. When it does, it is called **lava.** Over time, lava piles up. The layers of lava can form mountains.

It's About the Lava

About 1,500 of Earth's volcanoes are active. An active volcano is one that can **erupt,** or pour out, lava.

Some volcanoes make runny lava. This flows fast, like pancake batter. It piles up in thin layers. Over time, it forms low, wide mountains.

Other volcanoes erupt thick lava. This flows slowly, like toothpaste. It piles up in thick layers. Over time, it forms tall, steep mountains.

Real Fireworks. *Lava explodes as it hits the Pacific Ocean. The hot rock flowed downhill from Kilauea, a volcano in Hawaii.*

Busy Place. *TOP: Kilauea has been erupting since 1983. It is the most active volcano on Earth. ABOVE: Cooling lava forms rock. That is how the Hawaiian Islands developed.*

The Ring of Fire

Volcanoes are found all over Earth. Some form on land. Others rise up from the bottom of the ocean.

Most volcanoes are near the Pacific Ocean. This circle of volcanoes is called the **Ring of Fire** (see map).

Many volcanoes form where Earth's plates bump together. Plates are big pieces of Earth's surface.

NG MAPS

5

Living With Volcanoes

Many people live near volcanoes. Some live close to the base of the mountains. Some people farm nearby land. Ash from volcanoes is good for soil. So crops grow well.

Living near a volcano can be dangerous. Why? Volcanoes can erupt without warning.

Mount St. Helens Erupts

That is just what happened in 1980. On May 18, a volcano named Mount St. Helens erupted. Hot ash and steam blasted out of the volcano.

Few people were ready for it. Even scientists did not know it would happen that day. The volcano had not erupted since 1857.

Blowing Its Top. *An old photo shows visitors how Mount St. Helens looked before May 1980.*

A Dangerous Surprise

The burning ash poured down the mountain. It killed all the trees and wildlife in its path.

More than 20 years have passed since that day. Trees have now grown back. Animals live in the forests. Life has returned to Mount St. Helens.

Wordwise

erupt: to pour out lava

lava: melted rock erupted from a volcano

magma: melted rock inside Earth

Ring of Fire: circle of volcanoes around the Pacific Ocean

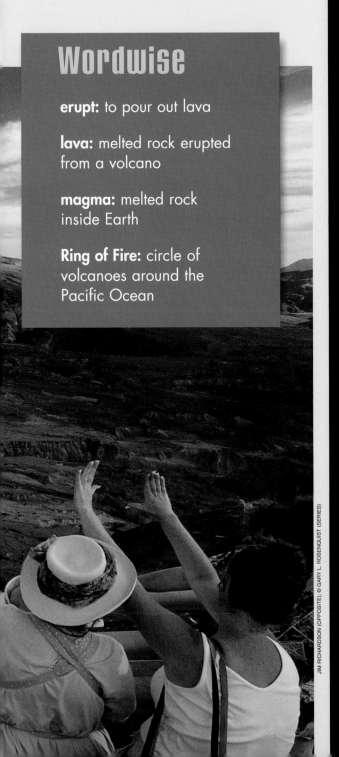

JIM RICHARDSON (OPPOSITE); © GARY L. ROSENQUIST (SERIES)

Mount St. Helens Erupts

MAY 18, 1980 • 8:27:00 A.M.
Picture–Perfect? *Mount St. Helens looked calm and peaceful. It wasn't. Scientists knew something would happen. But no one knew exactly when*

MAY 18, 1980 • 8:32:37 A.M.
The Bad Beginning. *The mountain exploded at 8:32 a.m. Ash soared 60,000 feet into the air.*

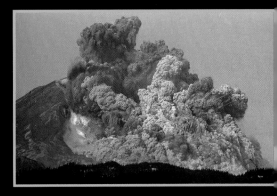

MAY 18, 1980 • 8:32:51 A.M.
Dark Day. *The blast produced 400 million tons of dust. It blanketed 230 square miles.*

Inside a Volcano

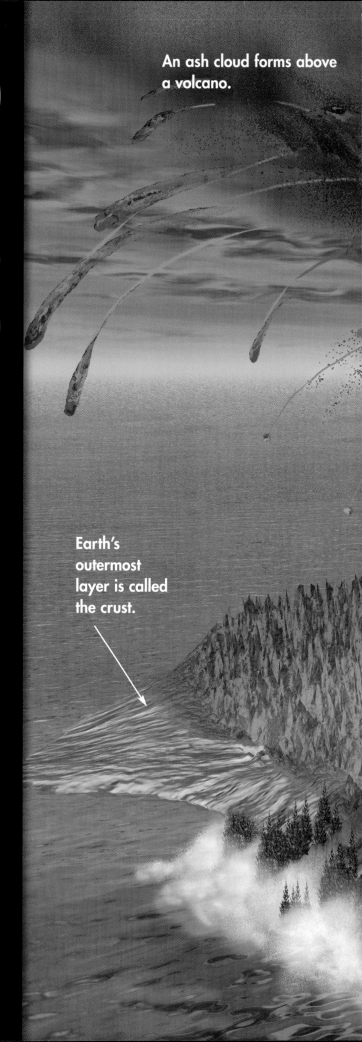

An ash cloud forms above a volcano.

Earth's outermost layer is called the crust.

Most people think volcanoes are big mountains that erupt lava. But a volcano really starts deep beneath Earth's surface, or crust.

The layer below the crust is called the mantle. It is very hot. The heat can melt rock. Sometimes pressure forces this heated rock through cracks in the crust. This can form a volcano.

Volcanoes form on all Earth's continents. They also rise from the ocean floor.

Use the diagram to learn about the different parts of a volcano.

Lava is molten rock that flows from a volcano.

A crater is the opening at the top of a volcano.

Molten rock rises through the central vent.

Magma is molten rock inside a volcano.

A magma chamber lies deep inside a volcano.

Hawaii
Island Chain

Hawaii is a chain of islands. They poke out of the Pacific Ocean. But there is more to Hawaii than what you see above the water. These islands are huge volcanoes. They rise up from the ocean floor.

Hot Spot

How did the islands form? Well, they sit above a very hot area of Earth's surface. Scientists call it a hot spot. The spot is so hot that it melts rock.

Volcanoes, Old and New

Millions of years ago, the hot spot burned a hole through Earth's surface. Lava poured onto the ocean floor. Over time, it formed a giant mound. At last, the rock poked out of the ocean. The island of Kauai was born!

Kauai was the first island to form above the hot spot. Over many years, a whole row of volcanoes formed. They are known as the Hawaiian Islands.

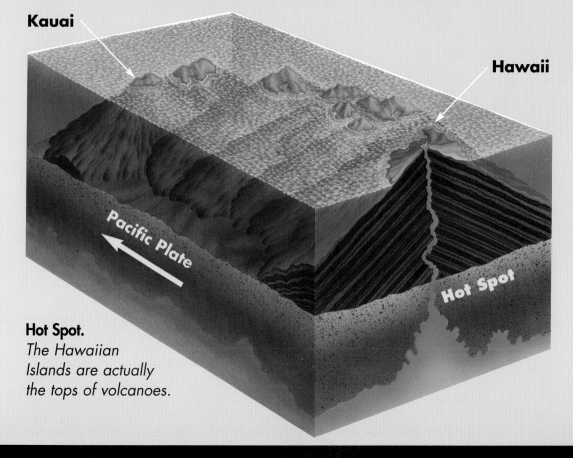

Hot History. *Kauai is the oldest of the Hawaiian Islands. This chain of islands formed over a hot spot on the ocean floor.*

How the Islands Formed

Kauai

Hawaii

Pacific Plate

Hot Spot

Hot Spot.
The Hawaiian Islands are actually the tops of volcanoes.

Volcanoes

Answer these questions to find
out what you have learned.

1 What is a volcano?

2 How is magma different
from lava?

3 What is the Ring of Fire?

4 Why might it be dangerous to
live near Mount St. Helens?

5 How did Hawaii form?

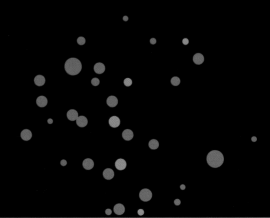